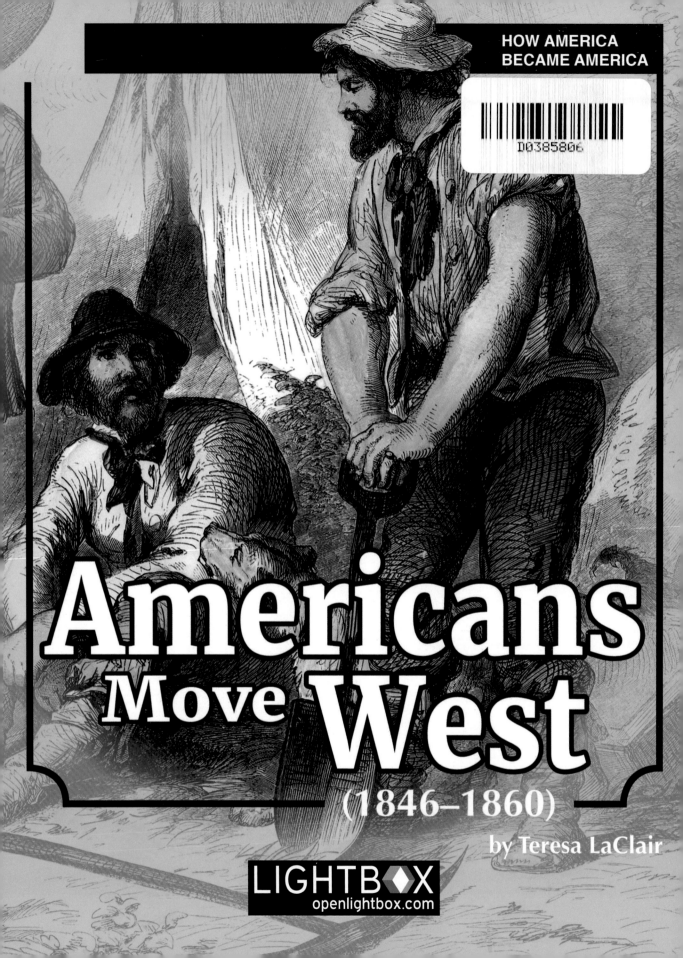

D0385806

Americans
Move West

(1846–1860)

by Teresa LaClair

LIGHTBOX
openlightbox.com

LIGHTBOX

Go to
www.openlightbox.com
and enter this book's
unique code.

ACCESS CODE

LBXP4322

Lightbox is an all-inclusive digital solution for the teaching and learning of curriculum topics in an original, groundbreaking way. Lightbox is based on National Curriculum Standards.

STANDARD FEATURES OF LIGHTBOX

 AUDIO High-quality narration using text-to-speech system

 ACTIVITIES Printable PDFs that can be emailed and graded

 SLIDESHOWS Pictorial overviews of key concepts

 VIDEOS Embedded high-definition video clips

 WEBLINKS Curated links to external, child-safe resources

 TRANSPARENCIES Step-by-step layering of maps, diagrams, charts, and timelines

INTERACTIVE MAPS Interactive maps and aerial satellite imagery

QUIZZES Ten multiple choice questions that are automatically graded and emailed for teacher assessment

 KEY WORDS Matching key concepts to their definitions

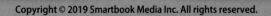

Contents

Chapter One

Manifest Destiny

The American people wanted to move west. They were excited about making their country larger. Politicians and journalists wrote that Americans had the right to spread into the West. And not only did they have the right to move west, they also had the duty. Americans believed they were supposed to expand their country. They believed that was what God wanted them to do.

One journalist, named John O'Sullivan, wrote that the United States had a "Manifest Destiny" to spread out across North America. The word *manifest* means "obvious, or easy to see." The word *destiny* means "meant to happen." "Manifest Destiny" meant that the United States was clearly meant by God to spread out to the Pacific Ocean.

Americans loved the idea of Manifest Destiny. They believed the United States was the best country in the world. They believed everyone should be free. They thought everyone should help govern the country—as long as they were white and men, anyway. These freedoms were some of the **ideals** Americans believed. They believed God wanted them to spread these ideals. Spreading American beliefs was their job in life, they thought.

People often represent ideals in human form. The idea of Manifest Destiny was usually pictured as a woman in a white robe leading settlers westward.

Manifest Destiny was a popular idea for another reason, too. The cities and towns in the East were getting crowded. A lot of Americans wanted space. Some people said that when you could see the smoke from your neighbor's chimney, it was time to move on.

People wanted lots of room to themselves. They wanted to move west. Manifest Destiny made them feel moving west was the right thing to do.

During the 1844 presidential election, James Polk ran for president against Henry Clay. Polk wanted to expand the United States. He wanted Texas to become part of the country. He also thought the United States should claim the Oregon **Territory**. Clay, on the other hand, didn't want to think about expanding the country. He thought Americans should focus on other issues. People were excited about expansion, though. They believed in Manifest Destiny. Even though not everyone was sure Polk would make a good president, he was elected.

Founded in 1788, Cincinnati, Ohio, was one of the American cities that grew quickly in the early 1800s. It had almost 25,000 people by 1830.

Before becoming president, James Polk had served in Congress and as governor of the state of Tennessee.

One big problem with Manifest Destiny was that the West wasn't empty. People lived there. Thousands of Native Americans already lived on the land. The United States had already forced thousands and thousands of eastern Native Americans to move west. They had pushed the Native people out of their lands in the East. They had sent the Natives across the Mississippi River. Now, Americans wanted the western land, too.

A lot of Americans argued that Manifest Destiny was a good things for Native Americans, too. They thought the Native people would be better off if they learned how to live the way Europeans lived.

Native Americans already had their own way of life, though. Their **civilization** was just different from the civilization Americans brought.

Some Americans thought the Native Americans should change to fit in with whites' way of doing things. If they didn't change, some people thought the Natives would become extinct, or stop existing. Some people thought that would be okay. They thought maybe Native people ought to become extinct.

Racism was a big part of Manifest Destiny. Racism is when one group of people thinks it is better than other groups. If the American settlers believed the Native Americans were their equals, they wouldn't be able to say it was okay to push them off their land. Most Americans at the time thought white people were better than everyone else. They thought their ideas and religion were better, too. They believed white people needed to help non-white people. Sometimes, they thought helping them meant killing them or making them slaves. They didn't think about things from the other point of view.

Not everybody agreed with Manifest Destiny, though. One politician, Charles Goodyear, said he hated hearing people talk about Manifest Destiny. He said he hated how Manifest Destiny had been used as an excuse for terrible violence and theft. Some other Americans felt the same way.

Some also disagreed with Manifest Destiny because of slavery. They thought slavery was wrong. They didn't like the idea of slavery spreading. They were afraid that if the United States grew, slavery would grow, too.

Most Americans did agree with Manifest Destiny, though. They believed they were supposed to spread out into the West. If Native Americans or anyone else tried to stop them, they believed they should fight.

In the election of 1844, James **Polk** received about **40,000 more votes** than Henry Clay.

By the late 1840s, there were 15 U.S. states that allowed **slavery** and 15 that did not.

Native Americans were not U.S. **citizens** until Congress passed a law in **1924** granting citizenship.

GET THINKING

Thinking about Manifest Destiny

Manifest Destiny provided a reason for Americans to settle the West, beyond their own personal interests. Some settlers may have felt sympathy for Native Americans. However, the idea of Manifest Destiny put the needs of settlers above those of other people. What do you think? Were settlers right to believe their needs were most important, even if Native people suffered as a result? Could settlement of the West have been done in a different way that would have been better for Native Americans?

Chapter Two

War with Mexico

On December 29, 1845, Texas became part of the United States. Texas had been part of Mexico. Now, Mexico was not happy. The Americans said the border between Texas and Mexico was the Rio Grande. Rio is the Spanish word for "river." The Mexicans disagreed. They said the border was the Rio Nueces, about 100 miles (160 kilometers) to the north.

The American president, James Polk, sent somebody to Mexico to talk about the problem. Polk didn't want to fight with Mexico. He wanted to solve the problem. The United States wanted to buy New Mexico and California. The man Polk sent, James Slidell, offered Mexico money for New Mexico, California, and the part of Texas between the Rio Nueces and the Rio Grande. Polk said the United States would pay the $3 million that Mexico owed to American settlers in Texas. That would be the payment for the territory.

The Mexicans were insulted by the American offer. They didn't think they owed the American settlers anything. And they had never given up their claim on Texas, either. They stopped doing business with the United States completely.

President Polk worried Mexico would start a war with the United States. He sent an army to patrol along the Rio Grande. General Zachary Taylor commanded the army.

Beginning in the 1820s, Americans used a wagon route called the Santa Fe Trail to trade, or exchange goods, with people in the settlement of Santa Fe, in the New Mexico region of Mexico.

On April 25, 1846, Colonel Seth Thornton was leading a group of 70 American soldiers. They were patrolling in southern Texas. The weather was very hot. They were looking for a place to rest and stay for the night. Their guide had told them about an empty **hacienda**. When they saw it, they headed for it. They were ready to relax.

When they got to the hacienda, though, they found it wasn't empty. Instead, 2,000 Mexican soldiers were inside. Nobody knows exactly what happened next. Someone fired a shot. Fighting broke out. For hours, the fighting raged. Sixteen American soldiers were killed or wounded. Finally, the Mexican soldiers captured the rest of the Americans. They took them prisoner and brought them back to Mexico. The conflict became known as the Thornton Affair.

President Polk was upset when he heard about the Thornton Affair. He went to Congress and asked that it declare war on Mexico. On May 13, Congress officially declared war.

Not all Americans were happy about the war. People in the Northern states were especially unhappy. They were afraid the war meant the South was trying to get more slave states.

The Mexican–American War took place in several areas. Colonel Stephen Kearny led part of the U.S. Army toward Santa Fe, New Mexico. He didn't want to fight a long and terrible battle. So he sent two men ahead to meet with the Mexican general in Santa Fe. When Kearny and his troops got to Santa Fe, the Mexican soldiers had gone. He wasn't sure what had happened. He never knew for sure, but he wondered if the men he had sent had bribed the Mexican general to leave. Whatever had happened, Kearny was able to take the city without having to fight at all.

Kearny got people together to govern Santa Fe. Then, he took his men and set out for California. On the way, they met Kit Carson riding east. Carson, a **trapper** and scout, was bringing news.

In Sonoma, California, American settlers hadn't wanted to wait for the U.S. Army to arrive. They had gone to Mariano Vallejo, the Mexican general in the area, and demanded that he surrender. Vallejo said he would rather California be ruled by the United States than Mexico. He asked if he could join the Americans. The Americans weren't sure about this, so they took him prisoner. Later, though, Vallejo would go on to become a California state senator.

Stephen Kearny announced to the people of Santa Fe that he would allow New Mexicans to vote for their government leaders.

The Americans in Sonoma made a flag. It had a star, a stripe, a grizzly bear, and the words "California Republic." What happened became known as the Bear Flag Revolt. The Americans declared California an independent nation. Less than one month later, U.S. forces arrived and claimed California for the United States.

After Kearny heard about the Bear Flag Revolt, he, Kit Carson, and about 100 men rode toward San Diego, California. Before they got there, they started hearing rumors about trouble. The Californios, Spanish-speaking people in California who had come from Mexico, were not happy about joining the United States.

When Kearny and his men reached the village of San Pasqual, just outside San Diego, they met a large army of Californios. They were outnumbered, but they fought anyway. More than one-third of Kearny's men were killed or injured. Eventually, American soldiers from San Diego arrived to rescue Kearny and his men.

On January 13, 1847, Kearny and the Americans were able to finally end the Californio rebellion. On that day, the Mexican governor in California, Andrés Pico, signed an agreement to stop fighting.

Kearny fought the Mexican-American War in New Mexico and California. General Winfield Scott, meanwhile, was marching toward Mexico City. The American troops led by Scott reached the edge of the city in September 1847. Over the next week, they fought several battles and captured Mexico City.

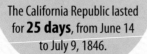

The California Republic lasted for **25 days**, from June 14 to July 9, 1846.

Between **8,000** and **12,000 Californios** lived in California in 1846.

About **10,000 American troops** died of illness in the Mexican-American War. About **1,500 troops** died in battle or as a result of battle wounds.

On February 2, 1848, Mexico and the United States signed the **Treaty** of Guadalupe Hidalgo. The treaty ended the war. In the treaty, Mexico also agreed to sell one-third of its territory to the United States. This land was called the Mexican Cession. It included the present-day states of California, Nevada, and Utah. It also included parts of Arizona, New Mexico, Colorado, and Wyoming. The United States would pay $15 million for the area.

As the Mexican–American War was going on, Americans were thinking about the Oregon Territory, too. At first, President Polk had wanted to claim all of the territory. That would have given the United States a huge piece of land reaching north to the southern border of Alaska. Finally, on June 15, 1846, the United States and Great Britain signed the Oregon Treaty. The treaty set the border between the United States and land that Britain claimed at the 49th **parallel**, which is where it is today.

Another piece of land was added to the United States in 1853. The country bought an area from Mexico that is now part of southern Arizona and New Mexico. This land was called the Gadsden Purchase.

U.S. troops led by Winfield Scott attacked Mexican forces at the Battle of Chapultepec in September 1847. The American victory was a key step toward conquering Mexico City.

Land Added to the United States from 1845 to 1853

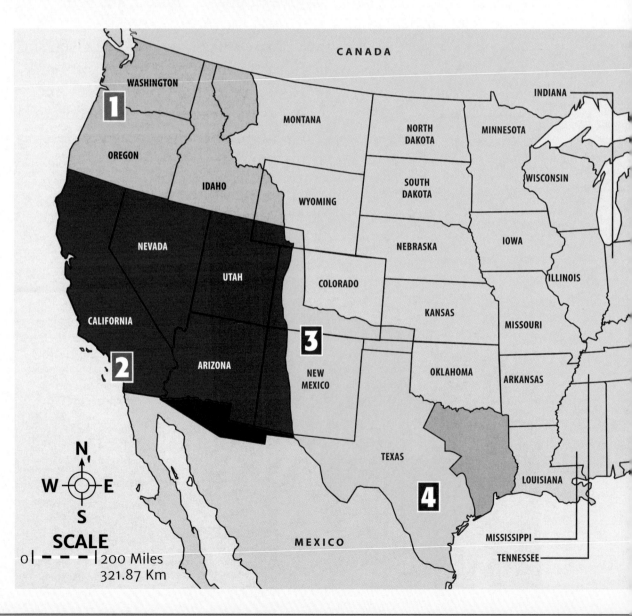

1 Oregon City

Trappers started a settlement at Oregon City in about 1830. After the 1846 Oregon Treaty, Oregon City became the capital of the U.S. Oregon Territory.

2 San Diego

Santa Fe was started by Spanish settlers in 1610. It is now the capital city of the U.S. state of New Mexico.

3 Santa Fe

San Diego was founded in 1769 as a Spanish mission, a settlement in which priests taught the Roman Catholic faith and European ways of life to Native people. About 650 Californios lived in San Diego in the 1840s.

4 San Antonio

San Antonio was the largest town in Texas at the time Texas became part of the United States. Today, 1.5 million people live in San Antonio, making it the 7th-largest U.S. city.

LEGEND

- ☐ Water
- ◻ Republic of Texas, 1845
- ◻ Oregon Territory, 1846
- ■ Mexican Cession, 1848
- ◻ Disputed area of Texas, 1848
- ■ Gadsden Purchase, 1853

Chapter Three

Why Americans Moved West

In the United States in the 1800s, moving west was a big deal. You had to leave your friends and family behind. You had to leave behind the life you were used to. If you lived in a town in the eastern United States, you would have stores nearby. You would have neighbors. You would have a school not far away. But life in the West was very different. It could be very hard.

People who moved west packed everything they owned into a wagon and set off across the country. They had to cross thousands of miles (km) of **wilderness**. Just crossing a river was hard. People died from hunger or sickness during the journey. Sometimes, they were killed by Native Americans. About one out of every ten settlers died on the trip west.

Manifest Destiny wasn't the reason people moved west. They wanted to move west. Manifest Destiny just helped them explain why they should move west.

One of the main reasons people moved west was because they wanted land. Farmers in the East felt crowded. Children from farm families grew up and wanted their own farms. But they couldn't always find enough land nearby. In the West, there was lots of land.

Newspapers wrote about all the land in the West. They drew pictures of happy **pioneer** families. They didn't talk about the dangers very much, though.

South Pass is a gap in the Rocky Mountains in present-day Wyoming. It offered settlers an easy way to cross the mountain range.

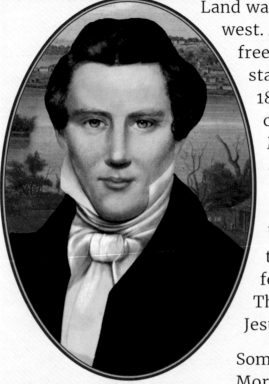

Land was just one reason people moved west. Another reason was religious freedom. The Mormon Church had started in western New York in 1830. Joseph Smith started the church. He said an angel named Moroni told him where to find a special book. Smith called the book *The Book of Mormon*. Smith told people about the book. Gradually, people started to listen to him. Together, they formed the Mormon Church. This is also called the Church of Jesus Christ of Latter-Day Saints.

Joseph Smith attracted followers from Europe as well as the United States. Members of the Mormon Church were called Saints.

Some people really didn't like the Mormons. They didn't like the things Joseph Smith was teaching. He said that a Hebrew family had traveled from Israel to South America thousands of years ago. He also said that all the Native Americans had descended from this family.

Other people didn't like the Mormons because their group grew quickly. They did business with other Mormons before they did business with non-Mormons. Some people thought they might hurt non-Mormons' businesses. Some also thought Mormons might take away many Americans' religious beliefs.

Sometimes, people who didn't like the Mormons destroyed their things. Sometimes, they threatened to hurt the Mormons. Because of this, Smith and the Mormons moved from western New York to Ohio in 1831.

The Mormons had trouble in Ohio, too, though. Their church kept growing. But so did the number of people who didn't like them. In the following years, the Mormons moved from Ohio to Missouri to Illinois. In Illinois, Joseph Smith was killed by people who didn't like the Mormons. Brigham Young took over leading the church.

Beginning in the 1840s, the Mormons traveled west from Illinois to settle in what is now the Salt Lake City area of Utah. They built the Mormon Trail. Along the trail, they set up places for travelers to stay. They built ferries to make it easier to cross rivers.

From Illinois, the Mormon Trail crossed the present-day states of Iowa, Nebraska, and Wyoming before ending in the region known as the Great Salt Valley of Utah.

A copy of John Sutter's sawmill stands at Marshall Gold Discovery State Historic Park in Coloma, California.

In 1848, people found yet another reason to move west. A man named James Marshall was building a sawmill next to the American River in northern California. Suddenly, he noticed something sparkling in the water. It was gold!

Marshall's boss, John Sutter, owned the land. He didn't want people coming to his land to look for gold. Marshall and Sutter agreed to keep the gold a secret.

Sutter had built a town called Sutter's Fort nearby, though. People in Sutter's Fort started hearing rumors about the gold. A secret about gold was hard to keep.

One man, Sam Brannan, owned a store in Sutter's Fort. Without telling anyone, he bought all the pickaxes, pans, and shovels he could find in northern California. Then, he collected a bottle of gold dust from the river.

Brannan traveled 85 miles (140 km) to San Francisco, which was then called Yerba Buena. He stood in the street and held up the bottle of gold dust. "Gold!" he yelled to all around him. "Gold on the American River!"

Soon, excitement had spread through the town. Everyone wanted to be rich!

Brannan had known what he was doing. Anyone who wanted to look for gold would need equipment. And Brannan had bought all the equipment. Everyone had to buy it from him. He made everything very expensive. A pan might have cost 15 cents a few days before. Now, Brannan was selling it for $8. In just a few weeks, Brannan made $36,000. Today, this would be millions of dollars.

People who reached California to search for gold the year after Marshall's discovery were called "forty-niners" because they arrived in 1849.

News of the gold took a while to spread across the country. People in the East heard rumors about the gold. They weren't sure if they believed the stories, though. Then, in December 1848, President Polk sent Congress his yearly State of the Union message. In it, he talked about the gold that had been discovered in California. He said a huge amount of gold had been found.

Polk's message convinced Americans the gold was real. Thousands of men left their families and raced across the country toward California. Others traveled by boat to California. They sailed around the tip of South America. They all wanted to reach California quickly, get rich, and then go home.

For most people, this plan didn't work at all. For one thing, getting across the country was very hard. Many died along the trails. They got sick. They drowned in rivers. Some were killed in accidents. Some people turned around and went home. The gold wasn't worth the trip for them.

By January 1850, nearly 40,000 hopeful gold miners had arrived in San Francisco by ship.

Miners used flat pans with water to search for gold in riverbeds. The gold was heavier than dirt, and it sank to the bottom of the pan.

The number of white settlers in California jumped from 13,000 to 300,000 between 1848 and 1854. Very few of them got rich. So many people had come looking for gold that most could barely earn enough money to pay for food and supplies. Some changed their plans and decided to open a store or laundry or barbershop instead. These people sometimes ended up a lot richer than the miners did.

Americans weren't the only people who rushed to California to find gold. People came from all over the world to get rich. The American miners weren't always happy about these people. There wasn't as much gold as people had thought. California passed a foreign miners tax. Miners who had come from other countries now had to pay a fee each month in order to look for gold. A lot of them gave up and went home. The gold wasn't worth the problems. It also became harder to find gold as time went on.

The Chinese were one group that succeeded in California. Instead of giving up and going home, the Chinese banded together. They helped each other. They built Chinatowns. These Chinatowns were like a little piece of home for the Chinese. Many men had left their families behind. They helped each other in their new country.

Many Americans didn't like the Chinese, though. The Chinese were willing to work hard and do jobs no one else wanted. They would sometimes take an abandoned mine and find gold in it. Other miners had thought the mine had no more gold. But the Chinese found gold that was hard to get out.

The number of Chinese men in California grew from 54 in 1849 to 116,000 in 1876.

California made the Chinese pay extra taxes. They had to pay the foreign miners tax. They also had to pay another tax that was just for the Chinese.

But they didn't get discouraged and leave. Instead, most of them stayed and made a life for themselves. Over the next 150 years, Americans accepted the Chinese and came to respect them.

The gold rush changed California in a lot of ways. Many thousands of people came to the area. Native Americans got crowded off their land. Forests were cut down. Streams were filled in.

The miners used **mercury** to get the gold out of the rock. The poisonous mercury killed fish and animals. It killed many miners, too. The mercury stayed in the land. It will stay in the rivers and dirt of California for thousands of years.

The Mormon pioneers, the gold rush, and the wish for more land brought people to the western United States. And these settlers changed the United States forever.

The Mormon Trail was **1,300 miles** (2,100 km) long.

More than **90,000 people** seeking gold came to California in 1849.

People mined about **12 million ounces** (373,000 kilograms) of **gold** during the California gold rush.

Chapter Four

Life on the Oregon Trail

*In April 1846, Mary Munkers and her family left Missouri. They were heading out on the Oregon Trail. She and her parents, her seven brothers and sisters, and the families of her three married brothers and sisters put everything they owned into covered wagons. Day after day, their wagons rolled across the **prairie**.*

One night, a storm blew up. Mary and her family huddled in their tents. Thunder growled. Lightning flashed. Drenching rain started to pour down. Suddenly, a wild wind pulled the tents open. Everyone was soaking wet! The men quickly ran from wagon to wagon. They tied them together to keep them from blowing over into the river. They tied the tents back down. All night the storm raged. Mary and the others tried to sleep.

In the morning, the storm had ended. The family checked to see what damage the storm had done. The wagons had survived, but their things had been blown all over the place. Mary and the family spent most of the morning gathering their belongings. Some things would be okay. Some were completely ruined.

The Munkers family was lucky. The storm was one of the worst things that happened to them on their way to Oregon. Many people weren't so lucky.

Pioneer families camped beside their covered wagons on the trail westward. Often, there was not enough space in the wagons for people to sleep in them.

The Oregon Trail was a popular route to the West. Thousands of people loaded their belongings into wagons and set out across the country. Most of them traveled in wagon trains. These were large groups of wagons that stayed together during the journey. When many people traveled together, they could help one another to stay safe and deal with problems.

The inside of a covered wagon had a floor and sides made of wood. Travelers coated the canvas cover with oil or paint, to make it waterproof.

A trip across the Oregon Trail took about five or six months. The really lucky people could make it in four months. When people ran into trouble, though, the trip could take even longer. A longer trip caused problems. A longer trip meant people had to deal with winter weather. It also meant they had to bring more food and supplies. Settlers who left Missouri in the spring had to travel between 15 and 20 miles (24 and 32 km) each day in order to reach Oregon before winter.

The Oregon Trail stretched for about **2,000 miles** (3,200 km).

The first Oregon Trail wagon train had **120 wagons**, with about **500 people**.

About **20,000 people** died while traveling the Oregon Trail.

The Number of People Who Moved West

Hundreds of thousands of people moved westward in the United States during the mid-1800s. Wagon trains began to use the Oregon Trail in 1843. By the late 1860s, traffic on the trail had decreased a great deal. Most people traveling to California in the gold rush arrived between 1849 and 1860. Most travelers who reached Utah by using the Mormon Trail came between 1846 and 1869.

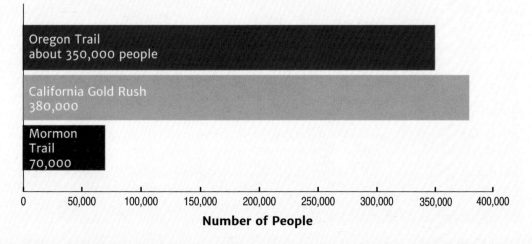

Oregon Trail
about 350,000 people

California Gold Rush
380,000

Mormon Trail
70,000

| 0 | 50,000 | 100,000 | 150,000 | 200,000 | 250,000 | 300,000 | 350,000 | 400,000 |

Number of People

The beginning of the Oregon Trail was in Independence, Missouri. Sometimes, people joined the trail farther west, though. Each winter and spring, people came to Independence. They bought supplies and got ready. They tried to bring everything they might need on the way. Most people bought oxen to pull the wagons. Oxen could pull a heavier load than horses. They were also cheaper.

Then, in late April or early May, it was time to leave. Everyone tried to get in line. Wagons got tangled together. Some people had never driven a wagon before. Driving a wagon could be tricky. Some people had trouble steering the oxen. Some even tipped over their wagons. All their things spilled out on the ground. They had to get the wagon back upright and reloaded.

Independence, Missouri, grew up around the courthouse on the town square. The town was located as far west on the Missouri River as boats carried people in the 1840s. This made Independence a natural starting point for the Oregon Trail.

Many times, as soon as people started out, they realized they had packed too much. The oxen had trouble pulling the heavy load. Most people walked instead of riding. Then, the oxen wouldn't have to pull them, too. But, even then, the oxen got tired quickly. The heaviest wagons fell behind the others. Just outside Independence, people who had packed too much started throwing things away. For a few miles, the trail would be lined with furniture, crates, and piles of food. People went through their wagons and dumped whatever they thought they could live without.

Before setting out on the Oregon Trail, a lot of people worried about being attacked by Native Americans. Really, though, such attacks were very rare. Native Americans were more likely to silently watch the wagons go by. Sometimes, Native Americans helped pioneers whose wagons had gotten stuck in mud or swept away by a river.

Native Americans who approached wagon trains often just wanted to trade with the settlers.

The real dangers on the Oregon Trail were diseases, accidents, and getting worn out from walking so far. The worst disease was cholera. Cholera was spread by dirty water or food.

People didn't understand that then. They only knew that sometimes people would be healthy in the morning and dead by night. They would suddenly get stomach cramps and feel very ill. People who died were quickly buried along the side of the trail.

Accidents killed a lot of people on the Oregon Trail, too. The most common accident was being accidentally shot with a gun.

River crossings were also very dangerous. Sometimes wagons were swept away when people tried to cross a stream or river. Deeper rivers often had ferries. These ferries were large flat rafts. Usually, the ferrymen took the wagons across one at a time. Sometimes, ferrymen tried to overload the ferries. This could be very dangerous. The ferries sometimes tipped over. Taking a ferry was also very expensive. Since everyone had to cross the river, the ferrymen could charge whatever amount they wanted.

Exhaustion was a problem for everyone, both people and animals. Even though most people walked, the wagons were still very heavy. Sometimes, the oxen worked so hard to pull the wagons that they died from exhaustion.

For years, the Oregon Trail was a big part of the United States. Thousands of people followed the route west. Then, in 1869, the last spike was pounded into the track for the country's first **transcontinental** railroad. Suddenly, people going west had a faster, safer way to travel. The days of the Oregon Trail came to a close.

People traveling in wagon trains elected officers to make important decisions. Officers rode on horseback and directed the wagons.

GET THINKING

Starting a New Life

Children who traveled the Oregon Trail with their families left their friends and homes behind. Many would never return to their former homes. How would you feel about leaving everything you knew and setting forth for a new life? What would you take with you? If you had to leave something on the trail during the journey, what would you choose to throw away?

Chapter Five

A Railroad across the United States

On May 10, 1869, a crowd of people gathered at Promontory Summit in Utah. They had come to watch the last spike of the transcontinental railroad be hammered in. Reporters waited. Photographers set up their cameras. The president of the Central Pacific Railroad Company, Leland Stanford, picked up a bronze and gold spike called the Golden Spike. The spike had been made especially for this moment. At 2:47 in the afternoon, Stanford pounded the spike into the railroad track. It was done! The railroad stretching across the country was finally finished.

Settlers had been traveling across the United States for years. Since the 1820s, American had been building railroads and trains. At first, a lot of people worried that railroads would be too dangerous. The first trains went about 15 miles (24 km) per hour. This was quite a bit faster than people were used to. Many people were too terrified to ride on the new vehicle.

Railroads became more common, though. People got used to them. Small, unconnected railroads were built in parts of the East. People kept talking about connecting the railroads and building a railroad line across the country.

The site of the Golden Spike ceremony was 690 miles (1,110 km) from where the Central Pacific Railroad had started building track east from California.

The idea of a railroad line connecting the different parts of the country slowly became more popular. But Americans disagreed about where the railroad should be built. There were three ideas.

Many in the North thought the railroad should start in Chicago, Illinois. This would mean it was closer to New York and Boston. These were two of the American cities with the most people living in them.

People in the South thought the railroad should start in Memphis, Tennessee. The South had a lot of big farms. But it didn't have very many factories. Southerners thought building the railroad across the South would help bring in more jobs and money. People in the North didn't like the idea of building the railroad in the South, though. They thought it would spread slavery farther across the country.

By the 1860s, New York City was the country's center of trade and industry. A transcontinental railroad would help New York companies ship goods to customers nationwide.

The third idea was to start the railroad in St. Louis, Missouri. This would be a middle option, between the other two cities. People in St. Louis thought building the railroad there made sense. The Oregon Trail already started in Missouri. It seemed only right to start the railroad there, as well.

Government leaders thought hard about all the ideas. They wanted to make a good choice. Finally, they decided to go with the central route. But instead of starting in Missouri, the railroad would start in Omaha, Nebraska. The Civil War was raging in the East. A lot of fighting was happening in Missouri.

Omaha had only about 2,000 people when it was selected as the eastern end of the transcontinental railroad. By 1890, the city's population had grown to 140,000.

On July 1, 1862, President Abraham Lincoln signed the Pacific Railroad Act. The act said the Union Pacific Railroad would start building in Omaha. At the same time, the Central Pacific Railroad would start building in Sacramento, California. The two railroads would build toward each other. Then they would meet in the middle.

In Sacramento, work started on January 8, 1863. At the end of that year, work started in Omaha. Six years later, the two ends were connected.

Finding workers to build the railroad turned out to be difficult. The work was very hard. The conditions were miserable. Working on the railroad could also be very dangerous. In 1865, the Central Pacific Railroad tried to hire 5,000 men. Nowhere near this many asked for the job, though. Of those who did come, 90 percent quit after a week. The work was too hard.

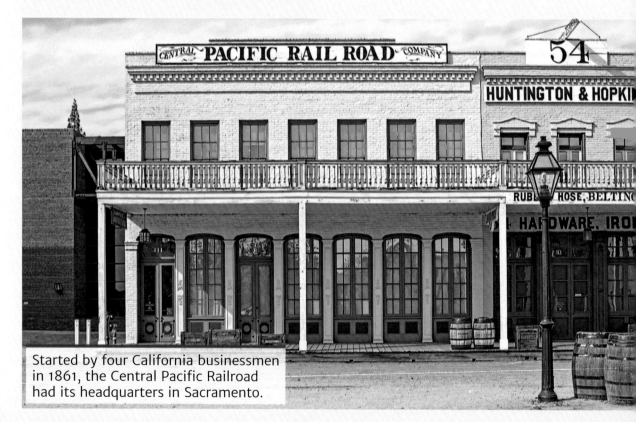

Started by four California businessmen in 1861, the Central Pacific Railroad had its headquarters in Sacramento.

After a while, someone suggested the railroad hire Chinese **immigrants**. The company bosses weren't sure that was a good idea. Most of the Chinese men were less than 5 feet (1.5 meters) tall. They didn't look strong enough to do the difficult work. Still, the railroad needed workers. So the company agreed to hire 50 Chinese men. The bosses were surprised when the Chinese worked harder and better than anyone else. They did the work well. They didn't complain. Quickly, the railroads hired thousands more Chinese immigrants.

Chinese workers used picks and shovels, wheelbarrows, and one-horse dump carts to build the railroad through the Sierra Nevada mountains in California.

Railroad workers on the plains often built track directly through land that Native Americans were using.

The transcontinental railroad made settling the West much easier. But it caused problems, too. The Native people had used the huge herds of bison on the plains for their food, clothing, and homes. But the railroad companies had killed thousands of these bison. The herds had become very small.

Settlers pushed Native Americans off their homelands. They forced the Native Americans to leave whenever they wanted their land. If they wanted it quickly, they sometimes killed the Native Americans who lived there.

By the end of the 1800s, most Native Americans lived on reservations. These reservations were small pieces of land set aside for them. The Native Americans couldn't move across the land as they once had. Their lives had been changed forever.

The new railroad built between Omaha and Sacramento was **1,776 miles** (2,858 km) long.

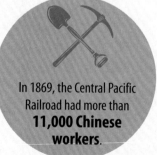
In 1869, the Central Pacific Railroad had more than **11,000 Chinese workers**.

The Central Pacific Railroad company built **15 tunnels** through western mountains to complete its share of the railroad.

The story of American expansion into the West has good parts and bad. The stories of the pioneers are stories of brave people facing hardships. But the effect on the land and on the Native Americans makes the stories sad.

Americans had great ideas about the world. They thought everyone should be free and able to decide their own lives. But these ideas didn't always work out. And there were always some people who had to give up their freedoms so that Americans could have theirs. Their stories got in each other's way.

GET THINKING

Railroads and a Changing America

The United States was only 50 years old when railroads began to be developed. The building of railroads was one of the most important changes of the 1800s. Do research to find out more about how railroads changed the United States. Focus your research with these questions:

- How did the railroad industry grow between 1840 and 1860?
- What forms of energy were used by locomotives in the 1800s?
- Why did some people oppose the building of railroads?
- What were some arguments in favor of the railroads?

Timeline

1843—Wagon trains begin rolling west on the Oregon Trail.

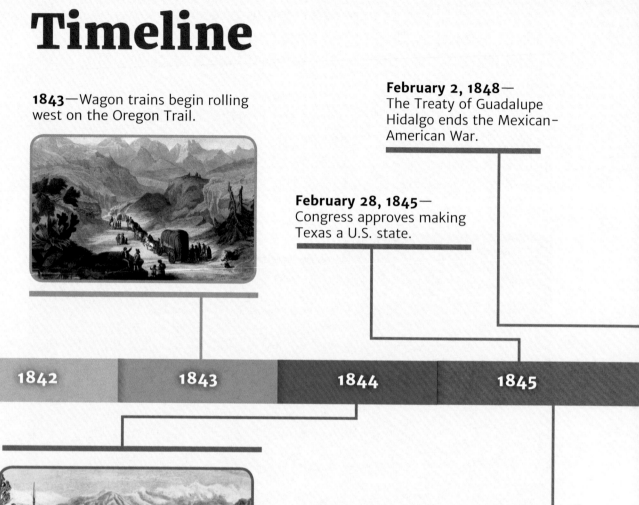

February 2, 1848—The Treaty of Guadalupe Hidalgo ends the Mexican-American War.

February 28, 1845—Congress approves making Texas a U.S. state.

| 1842 | 1843 | 1844 | 1845 |

1844—Led by Brigham Young, the Mormons begin moving to the Salt Lake Valley in Utah.

May 13, 1846—The United States officially declares war on Mexico.

1848—James Marshall discovers gold in the American River at Sutter's Fort, California, starting a gold rush.

1853—With the Gadsden Purchase, the United States gains 30,000 square miles (77,000 sq. km) of Mexican land.

| 1850 | 1860 | 1870 | 1880 |

1862—President Abraham Lincoln signs the Pacific Railroad Act.

1863—Work begins to build the transcontinental railroad.

1869—The transcontinental railroad is completed.

Quiz

ONE
What is the name of the belief that the United States was meant to expand westward?

TWO
In what year did Texas become part of the United States?

THREE
In which future U.S. state did the Bear Flag Revolt take place?

FOUR
How much did the United States pay for the Mexican Cession?

FIVE
Which religious group founded a settlement in present-day Utah?

SIX
In what year was gold discovered in California?

SEVEN
What was the length of the Oregon Trail?

EIGHT
In which town and state did the Oregon Trail begin?

NINE
In what year was the transcontinental railroad completed?

TEN
What is the name for pieces of land set aside for Native Americans?

ANSWERS
ONE Manifest Destiny TWO 1845 THREE California FOUR $15 million FIVE Mormons SIX 1848 SEVEN About 2,000 miles (3,200 km) EIGHT Independence, Missouri NINE 1869 TEN Reservations

Key Words

civilization: the way of life developed by a group in a particular time and place

hacienda: a name often used in Spanish-speaking countries for a home surrounded by a large farm or ranch

ideals: beliefs or goals that people work toward

immigrants: people who move to a country or area to live there

mercury: a silver-white metal that is a liquid at normal temperatures

parallel: a line of latitude, or an imaginary line around Earth used to measure distance north or south of the equator, the imaginary line around Earth's center

pioneer: one of the first people who settled an area

prairie: an area of flat grassland with very few trees

territory: an area that belongs to or is under the control of a government

transcontinental: stretching completely across a continent

trapper: a person who hunts animals for a living

treaty: an official agreement between two or more nations

wilderness: land that has not been settled by people

Index

LIGHTB◆X

➕ SUPPLEMENTARY RESOURCES

Click on the plus icon ➕ found in the bottom left corner of each spread to open additional teacher resources.

- Download and print the book's quizzes and activities
- Access curriculum correlations
- Explore additional web applications that enhance the Lightbox experience

LIGHTBOX DIGITAL TITLES
Packed full of integrated media

VIDEOS

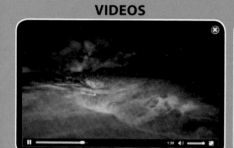

INTERACTIVE MAPS

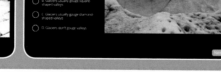

WEBLINKS

SLIDESHOWS

QUIZZES

OPTIMIZED FOR

✓ **TABLETS**

✓ **WHITEBOARDS**

✓ **COMPUTERS**

✓ **AND MUCH MORE!**

Published by Smartbook Media Inc.
350 5th Avenue, 59th Floor
New York, NY 10118
Website: www.openlightbox.com

First published by Mason Crest in 2013

062018
121117

Library of Congress Cataloging-in-Publication Data
Names: LaClair, Teresa, author.
Title: Americans move west, 1846-1860 / Teresa LaClair.
Other titles: Americans move west, 1846-1860 (Smartbook Media)
Description: New York, NY : Smartbook Media Inc., 2019. |
Series: How America became America | Includes index.
Identifiers: LCCN 2017054966 | ISBN 9781510536005 (hardcover : alk. paper) | ISBN 978-1-5105-3601-2 (multi-user eBook)
Subjects: LCSH: West (U.S.)--History--1848-1860--Juvenile literature. | Overland journeys to the Pacific--Juvenile literature.
Classification: LCC F593 .L17 2019 | DDC 978/.02--dc23
LC record available at https://lccn.loc.gov/2017054966

Printed in Brainerd, Minnesota, United States
1 2 3 4 5 6 7 8 9 0 22 21 20 19 18

Project Coordinator Heather Kissock
Art Director Terry Paulhus

Photo Credits
Every reasonable effort has been made to trace ownership and to obtain permission to reprint copyright material. The publisher would be pleased to have any errors or omissions brought to its attention so that they may be corrected in subsequent printings.

The publisher acknowledges Getty Images, Alamy, Dreamstime, Shutterstock, and iStock as its primary image suppliers for this title.